Y0-CAS-089

NOV 0 8 2010

MACHINES ON THE MOVE

HELICOPTERS

Andrew Langley

amicus

Published by Amicus
P.O. Box 1329
Mankato, MN 56002

U.S. publication copyright © 2011 Amicus. International copyright reserved in all countries.
No part of this book may be reproduced in any form without written permission from the publisher.

Printed in the United States of America, at Corporate Graphics in North Mankato, Minnesota.

Library of Congress Cataloging-in-Publication Data
Langley, Andrew.
    Helicopters / by Andrew Langley.
        p. cm. – (Machines on the move)
    Includes bibliographical references and index.
    ISBN 978-1-60753-059-6 (library binding)
    1. Helicopters–Juvenile literature. I. Title.
    TL716.2.L36 2011
    629.133'352–dc22
                                        2010006428

Created by Appleseed Editions, Ltd.
Planning and production by Discovery Books Limited
Designed by D.R. ink
Cover design by Blink Media
Edited by James Nixon

Photograph acknowledgements
Alamy Images: p. 13 bottom (David Gowans); Corbis: pp. 17 top (Tarmizy Harva/Reuters), 17 bottom (John Van Hasselt); Defence Images © Crown Copyright/MOD, images from www.photos.mod.uk. Reproduced with permission of the Controller of Her Majesty's Stationery Office: pp. 4 (PO Russell-Stevenson, Royal Navy), 9 bottom (Cpl Mike Fletcher, Army); European Air Crane: pp. 12, 13 right; Getty Images: pp. 16 (Sandra Teddy), 18 (Luis Acosta/AFP), 19 bottom (Alan Staats), 22 top (Time Life Pictures), 24 bottom (TG Stock/Tim Graham), 29 top (David McNew), 29 bottom (Tiziani Fabi/AFP); Istockphoto.com: p. 23 bottom; National Geographic: p. 23 top; Photolibrary: p. 19 top (Ted Kinsman); Shutterstock: pp. 5 (Maxim Petrichuk), 6, 7 top (Perry Correll), 7 bottom (Lucian Coman), 8, 10, 11, 14 (David Hancock), 15 top (Robert Kyllo), 15 bottom (Monkey Business Images), 20 (Chris Bence), 21 (Bruno Ismael Da Silva Alves), 22 bottom (Gaetano La Bruzzo), 25 bottom, 26, 27 top; Sikorsky Aircraft Corporation: p. 9 top (© Sikorsky Aircraft Corporation 2009. All rights reserved); US Navy: p. 27 bottom (Mass Communication Specialist 3rd Class Paul Perkins); Wikimedia: pp. 25 top (Bernhard Grohl), 28 (USAF).

Front Cover: Shutterstock: top (Sascha Hahn), bottom (Rob Byron)

DAD0042
32010

9 8 7 6 5 4 3 2 1

Contents

What Is a Helicopter?

A helicopter is an aircraft with no wings. The helicopter is lifted up by a spinning set of blades called a **rotor**. The rotor is like a giant **propeller**.

Rotor

A helicopter can fly freely in any direction. It can go straight up or down, and forward, backward, or sideways. It can even **hover** (stay still) in the air. Very few other aircraft can do that.

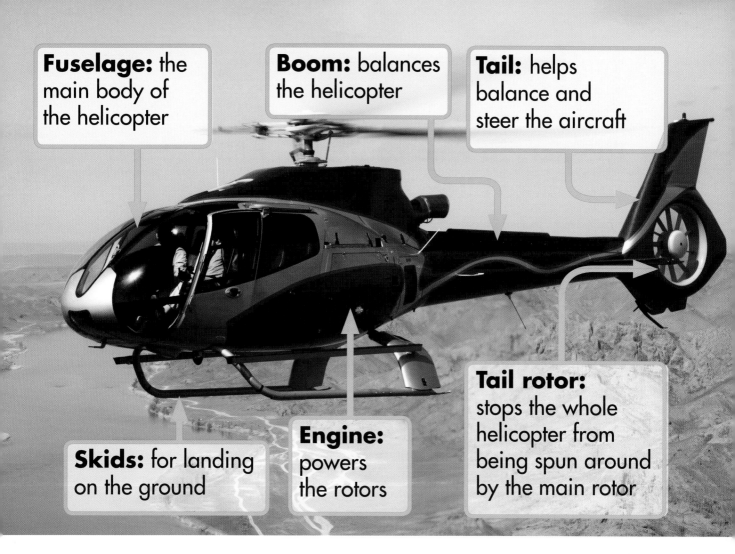

Fuselage: the main body of the helicopter

Boom: balances the helicopter

Tail: helps balance and steer the aircraft

Skids: for landing on the ground

Engine: powers the rotors

Tail rotor: stops the whole helicopter from being spun around by the main rotor

Rotor

The rotor has two or more long blades set at an angle. As the rotor spins, air travels farther over the top of the curved blades than underneath (right). This lifts the helicopter into the air. The pilot alters the angle of the blades to move the helicopter in different directions.

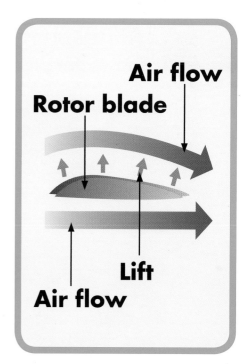

Air flow

Rotor blade

Lift

Air flow

At the Controls

The person who controls a helicopter is called the pilot. The pilot sits at the control panel at the front of the helicopter.

There are many types of controls on the panel. Levers and pedals move the helicopter up and down, left and right, or forward and backward. Dials and display screens show height, speed, fuel levels, and other vital information.

Altimeter: shows height

Rudder pedal

Cyclic control

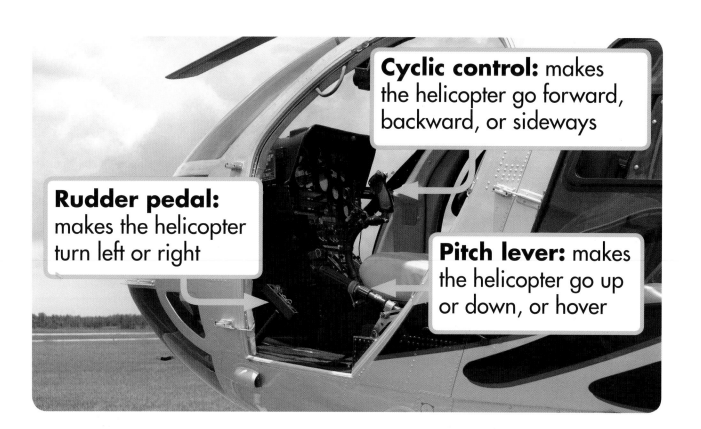

Cyclic control: makes the helicopter go forward, backward, or sideways

Rudder pedal: makes the helicopter turn left or right

Pitch lever: makes the helicopter go up or down, or hover

Hands and Feet

Flying a helicopter is a very skilled job. The pilot has to operate three sets of controls at once—two hand controls and one foot pedal.

Large and Small

Helicopters can take off and land without a runway. They have more uses than any other aircraft.

There are many different kinds of helicopters in the skies. The smallest can only carry one person (below). The largest helicopters have two rotors, and can carry very heavy loads.

World's Fastest

The world's fastest helicopter is the Sikorsky X2. It can reach a speed of 288 mph (463 k/h)—half as fast as a Boeing 747 jet airliner.

Twin Rotors

Helicopters with two rotors do not need a tail rotor to stop the aircraft from spinning around. The two rotors rotate in opposite directions. This keeps the helicopter straight.

Passenger Helicopters

Helicopters can land in a small space. They are great for carrying passengers over short distances or to places that have no large airfields.

Special landing areas for helicopters are called **helipads**. They are often in unusual places, from office or hotel roofs to offshore oil platforms.

HELIPAD KEEP CLEAR

Fuselage

The **fuselage** is the main cabin of the helicopter. All the other parts are attached to it. The pilot and passengers sit in the fuselage.

Into the Wild

Mountaintops or remote islands are very hard to reach by plane or land vehicle. But a helicopter can take people almost anywhere.

Flying Cranes

Helicopters are ideal for moving awkward and heavy loads. Special helicopters are used as "flying cranes."

These helicopters lift all kinds of loads, such as long sections of bridge and giant pieces of electricity towers. Because helicopters hover and fly **vertically**, they can set these items exactly where they are needed.

Sling

The load is lifted in a sling or a **cable** attached to the underside of the helicopter. The sling can be raised or lowered.

Aircrane

The S64 Aircrane is one of the strongest of all helicopters. It can lift and carry a load of over 9 tons.

Air Ambulance

An air ambulance is a helicopter specially equipped to pick up and transport sick or injured people. Helicopters can reach accident scenes faster than ordinary ambulances.

Landing Gear

Some helicopters have wheels attached underneath for landing on. This is called the landing gear. Others are fitted with two long bars, called **skids**.

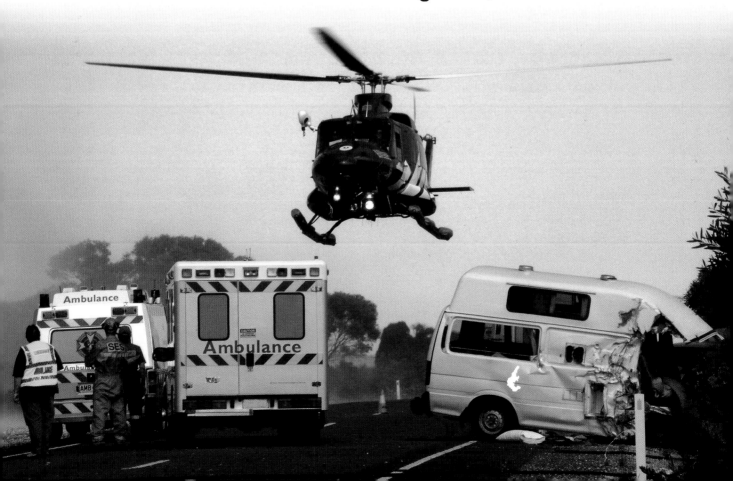

Care in the Air

Air ambulances can carry sick people from one hospital to another comfortably and quickly.

They are fitted with medical equipment, so the crew can treat the patient during the flight. Sometimes, a doctor carries out an emergency operation right inside the helicopter!

Emergency!

A sailor is trapped on a sinking ship. What's the quickest way to rescue that person? Send a helicopter!

Winch

Rescue helicopters have a **winch** fitted to one side. This is a cable that can be lowered to a person on the ground. The person is clipped onto the cable and is pulled up to the helicopter.

Emergency helicopters can rescue people from all kinds of dangerous situations.

Helicopters can also carry vital food and medical supplies to areas hit by disasters, such as earthquakes.

Mountain Rescue

In remote mountain areas, teams fly out by helicopter to search for and rescue climbers in trouble. The teams can even fly at night by using special navigation equipment and powerful lights.

Police in the Sky

Helicopters are very useful to the police. They give a bird's eye view of what is happening on the ground.

The police use helicopters to follow suspected criminals, even those in fast cars. The pilot can tell police cars on the ground where to go.

Heat Sensors

At night, police helicopters use **thermal vision** cameras to spot suspects. Color shows up on any object that is giving out heat—such as a human body (right).

Border Patrol

Smugglers and immigrants often try to cross borders between countries without being seen. Guards can spot them easily by patrolling border areas in helicopters.

Fighting Fires

Wild fires are a big danger in many parts of the world. Firefighters often use helicopters in their battle to put out fires.

Helicopters are used to patrol forests to watch for signs of fire. They can drop or spray water on the flames. They also carry firefighters to areas on the ground.

Helibucket

Helibucket

A helibucket is a strong, waterproof cloth bucket on a cable held beneath a helicopter. The pilot hovers and fills the bucket with water from a lake or the sea. Then the water is dumped onto the fire.

Flame Guns

Flame guns on helicopters are used to burn strips of forest ahead of the flames. This makes gaps that stop the fire from spreading.

Watching the World

A pilot in the air can see many things that we cannot see from the ground. That is why helicopters are used for watching from above.

TV crews cover news events from the air. On busy roads, pilots watch traffic and report jams or accidents.

Engineers in helicopters check railroad tracks, pipelines, or power lines for damage (above).

Onboard Computers

Today's helicopters have onboard computers. They work out information, such as the helicopter's position in the air and its speed. This helps the pilot stay on course and fly the craft safely.

Aerial Shots

Film and TV show producers use helicopters for shooting scenes. This camera is filming from a remote-controlled helicopter.

Troop Carriers

Helicopters have many roles to play in wartime. This is because they can reach places where ordinary aircraft cannot land.

Big, two-rotor helicopters carry troops, equipment, and ammunition. They can even transport **armored** vehicles. Awkward loads are carried in slings beneath the fuselage.

Biggest Ever

The Russian Mil V-12 was the biggest and heaviest helicopter ever built. It was 121 feet (37 m) long and 41 feet (12.5 m) high —as tall as a house. With a full load, it weighed 107 tons (97 t).

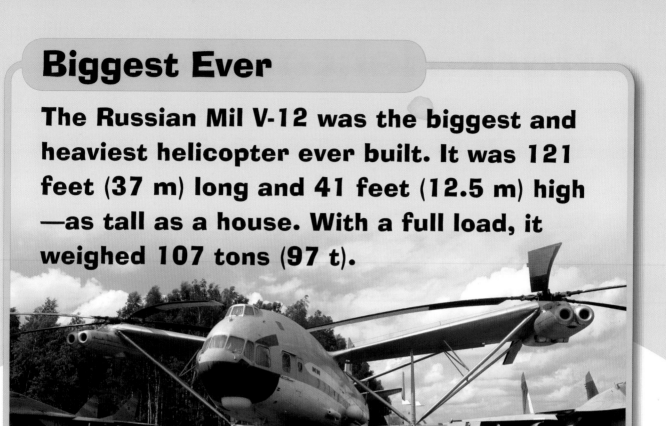

The Hatch

Most transport helicopters have a **hatch** at the rear of the fuselage for loading and unloading cargo. The troops below are about to make a parachute jump from the hatch.

Attack Helicopters

Attack helicopters have specially armored bodies. Military forces use them for self-defense and in times of conflict.

Attack helicopters strike at ground targets such as troops, tanks, and buildings. The **gunner** sits in a compartment beneath the pilot.

Weapons

Attack helicopters are fitted with rapid-fire cannons, as well as bombs and rockets. They can also fire **air-to-air missiles** against enemy aircraft.

Sub Attack

Navy helicopters have special equipment for finding and tracking enemy submarines under the water. They attack them with depth charges and torpedoes.

Future Helicopters

What will helicopters look like in the future? Engineers are working on new designs that will make them even more useful.

Designers are building **compound planes**. These can take off and hover like a helicopter, but fly forward with propellers or jet engines like an ordinary aircraft. The V-22 Osprey (below) tilts its horizontal rotors vertically like a propeller for forward flight.

Helicopters that can fly without a pilot (above) are being developed. They are controlled by people on the ground.

Backpack Helicopters

Backpack helicopters have two rotors, spinning opposite ways. The pilot is strapped in using a harness, and a parachute is included for safety.

Glossary

air-to-air missile a missile fired from a helicopter at another aircraft

airliner a large plane that carries passengers

altimeter an instrument that shows how high a plane is flying

armored covered with a layer of tough metal for protection

boom the structure fixed to the rear of a helicopter's main body that carries the rear rotors

cable a strong rope of steel or fiber (a power cable is one that carries electricity)

compound plane an aircraft that is a mixture of a helicopter and an ordinary plane

cyclic control a joystick that changes the angle of the helicopter's rotor blades as they spin. It is used to move the helicopter forward, backward, or sideways

depth charge a weapon that explodes when it is dropped into water

fuselage the body of a plane or helicopter, where passengers or cargo are carried

gunner member of a helicopter crew who operates the guns

hatch an opening with a door in the fuselage of a helicopter for loading goods and people

helipad a special area for helicopters to land

hover to keep a position in the air without moving in any direction

navigation the following of a planned course to a destination

propeller a set of blades spinning vertically that drive a plane forward

rotor a set of blades spinning horizontally that lift a helicopter in the air and drive it forward

rudder pedal the bar moved by the pilot's foot that changes the helicopter's direction

skids the long bars attached underneath a helicopter for landing

thermal vision seeing an object by sensing the heat it gives out, which then gives out bright color against the dark

vertically straight up or down

winch a machine for winding a cable up or down

Index

Web Sites

**www.williammaloney.com?Aviation/
AmericanHelicopterMuseum/index.htm**
Photos of different kinds of helicopters.

http://science.howstuffworks.com/helicopter2.htm
Watch these videos of a helicopter in flight.

www.exploratorium.edu/science_explorer/roto-copter.html
Make a paper helicopter and test it.